goSpeL
MEDITATIOÑS
for
MOTHERS

"Mother's Day and mom books can sometimes bring on the mom-guilt. Sometimes it can puff a mom up, making her quick to boast in herself. This book is for the weary and guilt-ridden, and the one who thinks she's doing alright. We all need the Savior and daily reminders that only God can establish the work of our hands."

—**Courtney Reissig**, author of *Glory in the Ordinary* and *The Accidental Feminist*

"*Gospel Meditations for Mothers* certainly strikes a chord to give comfort, empathy, direction, and sympathetic counsel to Christian mothers in our culture! Best of all, it points young and old alike to the Scriptures for ultimate guidance. These encouraging words answer questions as well as grab the heart to meet needs of everyday life. I loved it!"

—**Terry Pettit**, wife of Dr. Steve Pettit—together they have engaged in evangelistic, musical, and collegiate ministry for over three decades

"In the midst of busy days and sleepless nights, moms need the encouragement that only the gospel can give. *Gospel Meditations for Mothers* offers powerful biblical truth and guidance that reminds moms of the importance of their labors and cheers them on in their daily tasks. Whether you're parenting a toddler or a teen, these gospel-focused reflections will minister to your heart as you care for your children."

—**Melissa Kruger**, author of *Walking with God in the Season of Motherhood*

Introduction

The value of a mother is difficult to express without sounding clichéd. "The hand that rocks the cradle rules the world," it is said. True. And somewhat trite, due to its familiarity. But a mother's work *is* exceptionally important—and excruciatingly difficult much of the time. The physical price of carrying a child—of surrendering your position at the top of the food chain as you share your nourishment, your oxygen, and your very life with another for nine months—is surpassed only by the investment you make in that child for the rest of his life.

When Paul was looking for the perfect illustration of the deep affection and responsibility he felt for the Thessalonian Christians, he (and the Spirit) could do no better than the selfless care of a mother: "But we were gentle among you, like a nursing mother taking care of her own children" (1 Thessalonians 2:7). The allusion needs no explanation. Everyone who has ever *been* or *had* a mother just understands.

Joe Tyrpak and I fall into the latter category. We've had wonderful mothers. And we're married to wonderful mothers. Further, we pastor wonderful mothers. We're thankful for the opportunity to provide to mothers some instruction—and some much-needed encouragement!—along with our utmost respect and gratitude for your ministry.

This is our ninth collaboration in the *Gospel Meditations* series, and in this booklet we're blessed to have three guest contributors writing with us:

Hannah Anderson lives in the Blue Ridge Mountains of Virginia with her husband, Pastor Nathan Anderson, and three young children. She is a respected author, acclaimed for her two books, *Made for More* and *Humble Roots*. She is a contributor to The Gospel Coalition blog and one of the best examples of women who minister the Word to women with orthodoxy and artistry.

Angela Jeffcott lives in northern Utah, where her husband, Tommy Jeffcott, has pastored for ten years. Together they have three children, and Angela homeschools the two oldest. She is an addicted and aspiring writer who delights to focus her readers' attention on the themes of hope and grace with prayers for their growth and encouragement.

Tracee Veenstra is a proud mother, a joyful widow, and an engaging conference speaker. She and her family were blessed by *Gospel Meditations for the Hurting* during her husband's bout with cancer and her daughter's subsequent brain surgery, and her kind appreciation sparked a friendship. I remember gathering with my girls to pray for them when Tim passed away. In God's good providence, one of my daughters eventually roomed with Brooklyn Veenstra in college. Both mom and daughter have a resilient faith in Christ.

As always, our prayer is that you will find encouragement not merely from our words, but from the God-breathed Word, which alone is authoritative and sufficient. Read this as a guide to the Word, not a substitute for it. Be encouraged in your eternally important work. And thank you for your labor of love!

—CHRIS ANDERSON, EDITOR

Grace to You, Mom!

READ THE BEGINNINGS AND ENDINGS OF ROMANS – PHILEMON

"Grace to you. . . . The grace of our Lord Jesus Christ be with you." 1 THESSALONIANS 1:1; 5:28

It's tough to be a mom, especially in the early years. I often joke with people I see chasing a toddler: "It gets easier . . . in about ten years." Moms are often stressed, sometimes depressed, and always in need of rest. Always.

Sadly, a lot of moms make things even harder than they have to be. They're their own toughest critics. They live life under a cloud of guilt—from comparing themselves with other moms, from unrealistic books about non-existent Super-Moms, or even from well-meaning pastors and teachers who make normal moms feel like utter failures. Sure, I know there are moms who are passive and lazy—but they're probably not reading this book!

Mom, you of all people need to drink deeply of God's grace. Rightly understood and applied, God's grace is your spiritual oxygen . . . your lifeline . . . your only reliable coping mechanism.

It's no accident that the apostle Paul begins and ends his letters by saying, "Grace to you." Take a moment to look at the beginning and ending of every book he writes. Almost invariably, he offers his readers a blessing, praying for them to experience God's grace, and often God's peace. It's not just a sanctified salutation. It's more than a mere formality. It's a prayer. And it's a lesson. You—mom!—need grace, right now. Today. You needed it to save you from your sins (Ephesians 2:8–9). But you also need it to help you grow as a Christian—you will only grow if you "grow in grace" (2 Peter 3:18). And you need it to help you endure times of suffocating difficulty (2 Corinthians 12:7–10). Grace to you, mom. Sufficient grace to you!

How will you know if you're experiencing grace? Well, you'll be growing more and more like Jesus. You'll evidence the fruit of the Spirit. You'll resist besetting sins. But in your role *as a mom*, what are some telltale signs that you're enjoying God's daily provision of grace to you? Here are a couple practical indicators:

You won't spend your time berating yourself—for your imperfections as a mom, as a wife, or as a person. Such low-grade guilt or high-grade condemnation is from Satan, the Christian's accuser. He's got accusations covered—he doesn't need your help! When you're experiencing grace, you'll stop beating yourself up.

You won't constantly fret that you're ruining your kids. You'll relax. Do your best. Apply the Scriptures. But relax. There's a great mom in the church I pastor. She has four young kids, and at times her life is chaotic. During a recent parenting class, she once blurted out: "Let's be real. Some days a well-chosen Netflix video is the only thing that keeps me sane." We all laughed, and other moms looked a little less stressed. Letting a video or a game babysit your kids for a bit while you get dinner—or a nap—isn't the end of the world. When you're experiencing grace, you'll probably relax a little.

You won't be either so envious or so critical of other moms. You'll empathize with them. You'll pray for them. You'll laugh with them. But you'll neither exalt them as perfect moms (whom you kinda resent) nor deride them as pitiful moms (who make you feel a little awesome). When you're experiencing grace, you'll stop comparing.

You don't want to be a mom without God's grace. If your child's a toddler, you need grace. And when your child's a teenager, you'll need more grace. It may actually get more challenging in ten years. But there will be plenty left of grace. "Grace to you!"

Let the gospel strengthen you with God's grace for whatever motherhood throws at you today.—CHRIS

Love to the Universe and Back

READ 1 JOHN 3

"See what kind of love the Father has given to us." 1 JOHN 3:1

My eleven-year-old son is a bit of a mystery to me. I'm beginning to suspect that he always will be. He's more like his grandfather than either my husband or me. He's quiet and holds his cards close to his chest, taking everything in and letting very little out. His first-grade teacher called him an "old soul."

He's also a worrier, and he recently told me that he's decided not to be president when he grows up because the president has "a lot of problems to solve." When he shows me his schoolwork topped with As and glowing comments, he flashes a crooked grin but then drops his eyes. His confidence is fragile, as if he's afraid that something will sweep in and steal it away.

My husband and I try to meet each of our children where they are, to learn them, to receive who God has made them to be. But one night when I was tucking him into bed, he asked me something that made me doubt all of my parenting to this point.

"Mommy, do you love me to the end of the universe?"

I was stunned. *How could he not know? How could he not know that every time I look at him my heart bursts with joy? How could he not know that I love him?*

But then I realized that this was not about whether I knew I loved him but whether *he* knew that I loved him. And if he needed to hear it again, I needed to say it again.

"Oh honey, I love you to the end of the universe and back again. I love you just because you exist. And I will always love you. No mistakes you make, no bad things you do can stop me from loving you."

His lips slowly formed into a lopsided smile, and his blue eyes begged me to confirm that what he was hearing was true. He sighed and said, "Thank you for telling me that."

Then he rolled over and went to sleep.

If you've been a Christian for any length of time, you know that we talk about God's love a lot. When we're young, we sing "Jesus Loves Me" and learn John 3:16, the words tumbling off our tongues: "For God so loved the world. . . ." As we grow older, we can sometimes take God's love for granted, wanting to move on to more profound or practical insights. But for some of us, nothing could be more profound or practical than this simple truth: Jesus. Loves. Me. And He doesn't love me because of what I do for Him; He loves me because He is love.

If life with my son has taught me anything, it's that some of us need to be reminded of God's love. Some of us need to hear it again and again. So to you—you with the lopsided grin and expectant eyes—let me say this: When you doubt, when you wonder if God really does love you, all you need to do is look at the gospel. "For God so loved the world," John 3:16 continues, "that he gave his only Son, that whoever believes in him should not perish but have eternal life."

Let the gospel affirm God's love for you as many times as you need to hear it.
—HANNAH

Hour-by-Hour Satisfaction

READ ECCLESIASTES 1–2

"All things are full of weariness." ECCLESIASTES 1:8

Is daily life wearying? Do you struggle to find significance in your highly repetitive tasks? If so, God breathed out Ecclesiastes for you! Ecclesiastes is a deeply depressing and wonderfully clarifying book. It claims to be the work of a skillful literary genius, it claims that its painful considerations are from God and all for your good, and it claims to be all you need for constructing a healthy philosophy of life (12:9–12). So, you do well to experience its painful yet healing counsel.

Solomon opens the book with an observation on life: Everyone works hard, but nothing seems to change (1:3–8). No work seems to make a big difference. Isn't that a wonderful thought for parents? Your parents gave birth to you and raised you right. Why? So that you'll have kids and raise them right. And why are you having kids and killing yourself to raise them up right? So that they'll have kids and raise 'em right. A lot of wearisome work is taking place, but are we really getting anywhere? Are we just running like gerbils on a wheel?

What makes your life and life's work meaningful? In Ecclesiastes 2 Solomon explores three possible answers. First, he examines whether the meaning of life can be found in *pleasure* (2:1–11). He experiments with comedy and alcohol and beautiful properties and successful businesses and music and sex—and he discovers that living for pleasure leaves you empty. It's not what makes life meaningful. Second, Solomon explores whether life's meaning is found in *wisdom*—in figuring out how to make decisions that avoid obstacles and pitfalls (2:12–17). He discovered that, although wisdom is certainly better than foolishness, a wise person's life ends the same way that a foolish person's life ends: You die and are soon forgotten. Such a conclusion deeply disturbed Solomon—just like it deeply disturbs everyone who considers it. Third, Solomon discovered that, because everyone dies and ends up forgotten, a lifetime of *work* cannot give life its meaning either (2:18–23). These considerations led Solomon into painful despair (2:20, 23).

So, what gives your day-to-day life and work significance? Solomon ends the introduction of his book, chapters 1–2, with surprising joy. He affirms that there is "nothing better for a person than that he should eat and drink and find enjoyment in his toil" because these simple enjoyments are given "from the hand of God," and no true joy in life can be experienced "apart from him" (2:24–25). This passage is the first of numerous hints at the grand finale of Ecclesiastes, where Solomon teaches that the only thing that gives your life meaning is a personal relationship with the God who made you; this relationship allows you to receive with joy and thankfulness God's daily gifts of marriage and family and food (and coffee!) and work and sleep (12:13–14; see also 3:12–14, 22; 5:18–20; 8:15; 9:7–10; 11:7–10).

Solomon's depressing considerations in Ecclesiastes are designed to goad you to God (12:11). So many mothers are blinded, thinking that satisfaction in life is found in having loads of fun, making shrewd decisions, and working hard. Yet those things don't satisfy. Only God does. Scripture teaches that God Himself is the source of joy and pleasure (Psalm 16:11), that He gave you His Son to make your joy "overflow" (John 15:11), and that, when you submit to Jesus, He floods your work with cheerfulness (Colossians 3:23), your home with contentment (Philippians 4:10–13), and even your eating and drinking with eternal significance (1 Corinthians 10:31). Living *for God* floods your life with meaning and delight.

Let the gospel provide your life with meaning hour by hour and task by task.—JOE

Show the Joys of Mundane Christianity

READ GALATIANS 5

"Walk by the Spirit, and you will not gratify the desires of the flesh." GALATIANS 5:16

We live in the day of the superlative. Normalcy is so twentieth century. Everything today must be "hard core" or "radical" or "extreme," even in the church. (Bonus points if you spell it "Xtreme.") The push for Christians to take risks and get out of their comfort zones for the sake of gospel advance is good. But an unintended consequence of all the talk about "risk-taking Christianity" is that normal Christian people—including normal Christian moms—can be made to feel left out, selfish, and useless.

The truth is, Christianity has thrived for two millennia because of normal, faithful, and anonymous Christian men and women. For every heroic *martyr* in church history, there have been hundreds or even thousands of heroic *mothers*. Living a steady, even mundane Christian life isn't failure.

Have you ever considered the fact that the most common illustration for the Christian life in the New Testament is a *walk*? Over twenty times, in a majority of the New Testament letters, we are told to "walk" in a way that is fitting for Christians. The picture hardly needs explanation. To *walk* a certain way means to *live* that way—consistently, not occasionally. Step by step, day by day.

Walk in newness of life. (Romans 6:4)

Walk by faith. (2 Corinthians 5:7)

Walk by the Spirit. (Galatians 5:16)

Walk in love. (Ephesians 5:2)

Walk in a manner worthy of the Lord. (Colossians 1:10)

Walk properly before outsiders. (1 Thessalonians 4:12)

Walk in the light. (1 John 1:7)

Walk in the same way in which [Jesus] walked. (1 John 2:6)

Walk in the truth. (2 John 4; 3 John 3–4)

Walk according to [God's] commandments. (2 John 6)

The Christian life is a *walk*. You can't get much more pedestrian than that. It's not a high jump. It's not cliff diving, or bungee jumping, or parasailing. It's not all that extreme. It's just a walk—slow, steady, and sustainable. There are moms who are called to do exceptional things, like going to the mission field or adopting a needy child. Praise God for them. *Pray* for them! But don't believe the lie that your life is somehow meaningless if you devote it to raising your children, serving in your local church, and reaching out to your sphere of influence, as limited as it may be.

Mom, you have an amazing opportunity to show your children what faithfulness to their Savior looks like. You can show them genuine humility and unselfishness. You can model the fruit of the Spirit for them. You can teach them how to share the gospel with their friends—and pray with them for the salvation of those friends. You can help them strive for holiness without haughtiness. You can train them to love everyone and to abhor prejudice. You can help them see that being a regular and enthusiastic part of a strong local church is a joy, not a burden. Walk with them. Teach them the joys of a walk with Jesus. They may grow up to do amazing, radical things. And they may grow up to be normal, anonymous Christians for God's glory—which is a high calling indeed!

Let the gospel give meaning to your beautifully mundane life.—CHRIS

DAY
5

How to Clothe Yourself with Love

READ COLOSSIANS 3:1-21

"As God's chosen people, holy and dearly loved, clothe yourselves with compassion."
COLOSSIANS 3:12 NIV

....

"Put on . . . compassionate hearts, kindness, humility, meekness, and patience, bearing with one another and . . . above all these put on love" (Colossians 3:12-14). With these admonitions the apostle describes what mature Christian virtue looks like. What Christian mother can read such a list without deeply craving for such virtue to be increasingly characteristic of her life? But how do you actually put these virtues on? How do you, to use the illustration embedded in Paul's imperative, *clothe yourself* with Christian virtue? Paul indicates two ways which Christians often overlook.

First, understand how God views you. The most crucial way to clothe yourself with virtue is to understand your new identity as a Christian. Notice the little phrase in the middle of Paul's challenge: "Put on then, *as God's chosen ones, holy and beloved*, compassionate hearts . . ." (v. 12, italics mine). Before Paul tells the believers what "clothes" to put on, he tells them to look in the mirror. Paul wants the young believers at Colossae to know that they are elect, holy, and beloved. That is, they are chosen by God, set apart to God, and treasured by God. Those three terms were used both of Israel (Deuteronomy 7:6–8) and of the Messiah (Isaiah 42:1; Acts 4:27–30; Matthew 3:17). Paul uses the same three adjectives here to describe believers in the church. Incredible! If you are going to put on virtue, you're going to do it with the full realization that God the Father has set His love on you like He set His love on Israel, that He delights in you like He delights in His holy Son Jesus. See, you don't put on virtue hoping that God will choose you, but *because* He has chosen you before the foundation of the world. You put on virtue because God has already set you apart for Himself. You put on virtue because God already delights in you, *not* to make Him love you. Understanding your identity will *inevitably* lead to a changed life.

Second, imitate the God Who saved you. Paul's list of eight virtues in Colossians 3:12–14 is just a robust description of the capstone virtue—love. In other words, Christian love is compassionate, kind, humble, meek, patient, forbearing, and forgiving. (Compare this passage with 1 Corinthians 13:1–7 and Galatians 5:22–23.) So these virtues don't come one at a time but as a package deal. That really simplifies things. We don't really have eight items on our list—just one. So let's narrow our focus. Where does Christian *love* come from? It comes from God. God is love (1 John 4:7–12), and, when we personally trust the gospel, God pours His love into our hearts by His Spirit (Romans 5:5). Loving others is simply a trait of God's family—imitating God's fatherly love and Jesus' sacrificial love (Ephesians 5:1–2). So, Christian mother, if you want to clothe yourself with more and more Christian virtue, gaze on the glory of God. Gaze on His loving compassion to those in misery (Romans 12:1). Gaze on the loving kindness of God that appeared on earth to save the foolish (Titus 3:3–5). Gaze on the loving humility of God that made Himself nothing for your sake (Philippians 2:1–11). Gaze on the loving meekness of your King (Matthew 11:29; 21:5). Gaze on God's loving patience toward rebels (1 Timothy 1:16) and His loving forbearance amidst all your offenses (Romans 2:4). Gaze on the massive amount of debt you owed God that He lovingly canceled when you pleaded for His forgiveness (Luke 7:36–50).

If you are craving more patience with your children, more forbearance toward your husband, and more humility in daily conversation, take time to more deeply internalize the gospel. Understand who you are since you trusted Jesus and imitate the character of the One Who saved you.

Let the gospel motivate and enable you to put on virtue.—JOE

Fear Not

READ 1 JOHN 4:7–21

"In God, whose word I praise, in God I trust; I shall not be afraid." PSALM 56:3–4

Do you remember what you were afraid of when you were a child? Common childhood fears include darkness, monsters, or being alone. I always thought when I grew up my fears would leave. As I got used to sleeping without a nightlight and realized monsters weren't real, I imagined myself free from worries.

But adulthood brings a whole different set of fears with it, fears that only expand in motherhood. Suddenly you are responsible to raise, nurture, protect, feed, watch over, and care for someone who can do nothing without you. I remember many naptimes when I would stand over my newborn, watching her sleep, overwhelmed with the reality of being a mother, fearful I would somehow fail that tiny girl lying in the crib.

The Bible speaks to the fear and worry that all moms face. It shows us two types of fear, one good and one bad. The first is the fear of God (Psalm 2:11, 67:7; Deuteronomy 6:13). This fear is a reverential or "in-awe-of" fear. We see who we are compared to our all-knowing Creator, and we marvel at Who He is because He is so far above us. Mary, the mother of Jesus, gives us an example of this reverential fear in her prayer in Luke 1:50: "His mercy is for those who fear him."

But there is a second type of fear that we are warned about. This fear is being anxious or afraid about things we can't control or predict. When we look at our world and imagine what it will be like for our children in the coming years, it's difficult to not be anxious. But think about what worrying does to us. It robs us of joy because we don't focus on the good we have. It keeps us from sleep and rest, altering our physical and mental abilities. But most importantly, it makes our concerns more important to us than trusting the God Who is powerful enough to help with them. This second type of fear keeps us from the first; it keeps us from fearing the Lord the way we should.

When we worry about how our children will grow up or how we'll provide for what they need, we are in essence telling God that we don't believe He will oversee them. But if you have a proper fear of God, then you know that nothing is outside of His control. You can "cast your anxieties on him," as Peter says, "because He cares for you" (1 Peter 5:7). That's also why Jesus instructs us to not worry about tomorrow: because God will take care of it (Matthew 6:25–34; Luke 12:6–7, 22–32).

Fear and its hold on us was destroyed at the cross. When we fix our mind on Jesus and the sacrifice He made for us there, we can rest in His loving care. The God Who overcame death can also provide, protect, lead, and comfort us through all our lives. It takes a daily reminder to lean on God and not let fear control our minds, but He has promised to care for us just as a shepherd cares for his sheep (Psalm 23; Isaiah 40:11).

Solomon's direct counsel is precisely what we need: "In the fear of the LORD one has strong confidence, and his children will have a refuge" (Proverbs 14:26). May the Lord help us to fear Him . . . and nothing else.

Let the gospel remind you there is no need to fear because of Christ.—ANGELA

How to Raise a Pharisee
READ MATTHEW 23

"Woe to you, scribes and Pharisees, hypocrites! For you . . . outwardly appear righteous to others, but within you are full of hypocrisy and lawlessness." MATTHEW 23:27–28

Every mother has dreams about the future vocation of her children. Mom may want Junior to grow up to be a doctor, a teacher, or a missionary. While few would admit it out loud, some are absolutely *determined* to see Junior grow up to be a Pharisee, and they have a thorough training regimen to make that goal a reality. Here are several nearly fool-proof ways to raise Pharisees:

Teach them they are very good and that others are very bad. The Pharisees of Jesus' day were noted for their self-righteousness. They congratulated themselves on their goodness and condemned those whom they deemed to be sinners (Luke 15:1–2; 18:9–14). They didn't benefit from Christ's work to save them because they didn't see the need—they believed they were already spiritually "fit as a fiddle" (Matthew 9:10–13). If you want your children to eschew grace and embrace a works-based religion, congratulate them on their goodness even as you condemn other children in your neighborhood and church in front of them. Works every time!

Teach them to keep the rules, no matter what. You'll never succeed in raising a true legalist unless you train them that rule-keeping is the secret to godliness. The smaller the rule, the more important it becomes (Matthew 23:23). Have a long list of "to-dos" and "taboos." Maximize external matters as tell-tale signs of either godliness or compromise, while minimizing the condition of their hearts. Teach them to scrutinize those who seem to be serving the Lord but don't follow your list of rules (Luke 13:14). Remind them that the "cup" and "tomb" of their lives don't need to be internally clean, as long as they *look* clean (Matthew 23:25–28).

Teach them to value approval and appearances. Teach them to love—indeed to *seek*—the praise of men (Matthew 6:1–2, 5, 16). Teach them to learn the art of the spiritual "humble brag." Show them that it is sometimes necessary to alter their behavior (or perceived behavior) so that one who disapproves of them will be won over. Make them absolutely *captive* to the opinions of others. Sanctify this fear of man by calling it their "testimony." Of course, at times that will mean deceiving others to keep up appearances. Teach them that your family's reputation must be preserved at all costs. For example, tell them that while your family might secretly enjoy a certain movie or television show, they must never *mention* that fact to people at church. Teach them to be clever that way. They'll get it! Hypocrisy is vital to the development of your budding Pharisee (Matthew 23:13, 15, 23, 25, 27, 29).

Teach them that God's approval depends on their performance. Above all, teach them that God will accept them only if they behave, at least in the ways you've delineated for them (Matthew 23:13). Don't just teach them; *show* them! Tell them you love them and are proud of them only when you think they deserve it. When they don't measure up, make them feel like outcasts (Luke 19:7). Condemn them. Withhold mercy. Teach them that God will do the same. It's essential that they equate God's approval and man's. If pastors and teachers think they're holy, God surely must. Be sure they live under constant pressure to earn God's favor by their performance, lest they be like the wretched sinner who confessed his sins to God and was therefore justified (Luke 18:9–14).

If, on the other hand, you want to raise children who value the grace of God as extended to them through the finished work of Jesus—well, *taking this advice will do you no good whatsoever.*

Let the gospel help you point your children away from works to Jesus' grace.—CHRIS

Patient to Salvation

READ 2 PETER 3

"And count the patience of our Lord as salvation." 2 PETER 3:15

When I misbehaved as a child, my father did not become angry or violent. He never roared, strutted, or flaunted his authority. He didn't yell or belittle me. When I failed, he didn't condemn. He was excruciatingly patient and self-possessed.

It was terrifying.

In fact, my most uncomfortable childhood memories are sitting across from him after he caught me doing something I shouldn't. Silent, he would simply look at me and wait. I dare not say anything either. One thing I had learned through these encounters was that talking only got me into trouble.

Eventually he would break the silence by saying simply, "Tell me what you did." This was my cue. Predictably, I began with "I didn't do anything." Then I'd confidently rehearse my version of events and, more often than not, conclude with an outright lie. He'd listen, sit silently for another few minutes, and then repeat, "Tell me what you did."

So for a second time, I'd tell my story, perhaps revise a few facts, and add a detail of truth, hoping to convince him. But he was too smart for that. He'd listen and again say, "Tell me what you did."

By this point I'd be frustrated. *Was he deaf? I'd just told him twice what had happened. What more could I say? This was getting us nowhere.* But I had no choice, so I'd repeat my excuse for a third time. And still all he would say was, "Tell me what you did."

Frustration would turn to anger. *How dare he sit there so passively, so silently! If he doesn't believe me, he should at least say so, get angry, and threaten me. We both know I'm guilty; we both know I deserve to be punished—why doesn't he just do something!* I don't remember how long we'd sit there, him listening patiently while I talked myself in circles, but I do remember that the truth always cycled its way out of the lie—sometimes purposefully, often not. Eventually my own lips would condemn me.

Then, and only then, my father would speak. He would speak words of correction and discipline, but he also spoke of his own past failures and of forgiveness—forgiveness that until then I didn't even know I needed. This was the power of my father's self-possession—his patience forced me to wrestle with my own guilt, and in doing so, prepared me to receive mercy that I couldn't have only moments before.

Some might see such patience as weakness. In fact, that's exactly the reasoning of those who scoff at the Lord's longsuffering in extending His coming judgment. It hasn't happened yet, they reason, so it must not be going to happen. They see God's patience and count it as impotence. Peter corrects such foolish thinking: "The Lord is not slow to fulfill his promise as some count slowness, but is patient toward you, not wishing that any should perish, but that all should reach repentance. . . . [Therefore]count the patience of our Lord as salvation" (vv. 9, 15).

We expect God to deal with our sin immediately—to rant and rave and hurl down condemnation—only to find that He doesn't. He calmly waits and uses many different means to allow us to come face to face with our guilt. And once we've worked through our reserve of excuses, when we finally realize that we need Him, He stands ready to overwhelm us with grace and forgiveness. A grace and forgiveness that comes to us through Christ who bore the wrath on the cross.

Let the gospel remind you that God's patience leads us to repentance.—HANNAH

Take Care of Yourself

READ EPHESIANS 5:16–6:4

"Be filled with the Spirit." EPHESIANS 5:18

If you've ever flown in an airplane, you know the drill recited as a pre-departure announcement: "If the cabin loses air pressure, oxygen masks will deploy. Place the mask over your nose, securing it with the elastic band. Even if the bag does not inflate, oxygen will begin to flow." The last portion of the announcement instructs you to put on your own mask before helping your child with hers. That's good advice for life, not just for flights. A passed-out momma is no help to anybody. You need spiritual oxygen if you're going to be a help to your family.

Ephesians 5:22–24 tells you the kind of wife you should be.

Ephesians 6:4 tells you (along with your husband) what kind of parent to be.

Good luck with that. You can't do it—neither one. It's not in you to be a submissive and supportive wife, much less an even-tempered and instructive mother. Your family is maddening at times. You're maddening at times. Both passages would be absolutely suffocating if not preceded by the divine oxygen that makes obeying them possible. Thankfully, Ephesians begins with 1:1, not 5:22 or 6:4.

Ephesians 1–3 gives you the "oxygen mask" of the gospel. Were it not for the gospel, you would still be "dead in trespasses and sins" (2:1), a slave of Satan's suggestions and your own passions (2:2–3). Praise God for the divine intervention contained in two remarkably pregnant words: "But God" (2:4). Ephesians 1–3 is a treasure chest of the blessings that are yours in the gospel. Through the work of Jesus Christ, you have been brought from death to life. Redeemed. Forgiven. Reconciled. Everything about you has been changed by the miracle of the new birth. This is crucial for you to understand. If you were still dead in sin, you couldn't be a good wife. You couldn't be a good mother. But because of what Christ has accomplished on your behalf, you have the spiritual life needed to be a faithful wife and mom. You are a new person—delivered from the despotism of Satan and self and freed to the liberty of grace-enabled obedience. The gospel frees you from your sin and frees you to be a godly woman, and wife, and mom.

Ephesians 5:18 gives you the "oxygen" of the empowering Holy Spirit. The gospel brought you to life. But God didn't leave you on your own, even as a new creation. God has done even more, giving you the indwelling, controlling, enabling influence of the Holy Spirit. Your life may be animated by the moment-by-moment energy of God the Spirit. The point of the command to "be filled with the Spirit" isn't that you need to obtain Him. You already have Him if you're a Christian. But He must have you. The issue is control. The Spirit of God resides in you; Ephesians 5:18 is commanding you to allow Him to be the "Driver" rather than the "Passenger." Be altered by the Spirit's control. Let Him change your thinking, behavior, and impulses so that they are selfless and godly rather than selfish and fleshly. Be controlled by the Spirit! That's the oxygen for your spiritual life, enabling you to be a godly wife and mom.

Much of a mother's life is spent caring for the needs of others. But put on your own spiritual oxygen mask first, mom. Get your time in the Word every day, even if it means using an iPad as a babysitter for a bit. Breathe deeply of gospel truth. Fill your spiritual lungs with grace. Yield to the indwelling Spirit of God, gaining from Him the ability to do what you ought.

Let the gospel that brought you to life enable you to be a flawed but effective mom.
—CHRIS

Motherhood Is a Marathon

READ HEBREWS 11:11–12:2

"You have need of endurance." HEBREWS 10:36

My mom is a hero in my eyes. She's also a hero in my siblings' eyes. See, I'm the middle child of eight—My oldest brother is ten years older than me and my youngest brother is ten years younger. Yes, you did the math right. My mom had at least one infant or toddler in the house for a few decades of her life! And all of us kids are amazed by her. Now that I and all my siblings are adults and have children of our own, we often tell her, "Mom, you're incredible! We can barely keep our heads above water with *four* children—not to mention *eight*! How did you do it?" Her simple, honest answer is this: "There are about twenty years of my life that I don't remember; they're a blur." (Mind you, my mother was a teetotaler.) As she sought to raise her kids to love Jesus (often singlehandedly because Dad's work frequently took him out of town), she was in constant demand and beyond exhausted—pretty much every day.

Motherhood is a marathon, not a sprint. Like a marathon, motherhood involves enduring when you're exhausted, enduring when you're aching, and enduring when you can't imagine how you're ever going to make it across the finish line. Motherhood involves numerous hardships, including (at least) sleepless nights, rebellious kids, and incessant menial responsibility. For many mothers, there are added hardships such as cabin fever (during long, cold winters or long, hot summers), criticism, singleness, and children with special needs. In addition, the marathon of motherhood involves common besetting sins—Some moms try to *escape* their responsibility through binge watching; others try to *dull* the marathon's pain through exorbitant spending or through excessive eating and drinking; still others tend to stoically *absorb* their hardships, allowing themselves to become spiritually hardened and deeply embittered at God and others in the process. Motherhood is a marathon. How can you endure?

The writer to the Hebrews likens the whole Christian life to a marathon with his vivid words in the twelfth chapter: "Since we are surrounded by so great a cloud of witnesses, let us also lay aside every weight, and sin which clings so closely, and let us run with endurance the race that is set before us" (12:1). As in a marathon, few things in the Christian life are of greater encouragement than examples of those who've experienced the hardships you're experiencing and made it through. In this brief encouragement, the writer urges struggling Christians to consider the "huge crowd of witnesses" (NLT)—believers who endured trial upon trial by nothing but faith in the Lord. He urges you to consider (among others) Abraham and Sarah, Moses and Rahab. Then the author encourages you to consider Jesus.

Jesus is the preeminent *Example*, ultimate *Object*, and final *Reward* of your faith. Look to Jesus as the *Example* of faith because He fixed His own heart on trusting His Father, and that allowed Him to endure greater suffering than you and I will ever know. Look to Jesus as your faith's *Object* because, as this entire letter unpacks, He is God's perfect Son who became the perfect Man, He is the perfect Leader of God's people, He is the perfect and eternal High Priest, He is the perfect Mediator of the covenant that can make you perfect, and He Himself is the perfect once-for-all Sacrifice for sin. Look to Jesus as your faith's *Reward* because, when your race is done, you will see His face, enter His kingdom, and experience His unending joy.

Mom, "run with endurance." Fix your eyes on Jesus. You'll cross the finish line (both the finish line of motherhood and the finish line of the Christian life) and join the crowd of faithful heroes cheering others on to worth-it-all endurance.

Let the gospel of Jesus' self-sacrificial endurance lead you to endure.—JOE

Abounding in Hope through Trial and Loss
READ PROVERBS 3

"Trust in the LORD *with all your heart, and do not lean on your own understanding."* PROVERBS 3:5

We decided to wait until our daughter's performances in the school play had ended to break the news. On Mother's Day 2015 I could hear myself speaking, but I still wasn't grasping the words: "Sweetheart, Dad has been diagnosed with cancer." In that instant, her world was turned upside down, just like ours had been ten days prior. The following morning's surgery would reveal what we didn't want to hear—the cancer was advanced.

Brooklyn had always been a daddy's girl who adored going on "ventures" with him. The next twelve months would be the adventure we never anticipated. As we reflect back, we thank God for His sovereign plan: Although she had been disappointed not to graduate with her class due to health issues (see Day 20), only God could have known that later we would be praising Him for His perfect plan in allowing her to be right where she needed to be during her dad's illness.

Cancer can be explained as both brutal and beautiful—brutal because of the horrific effects of the disease on the body, but beautiful because you have a front-row seat to God's grace in action. "Strength for today and bright hope for tomorrow," a line from "Great is Thy Faithfulness," became our family's anthem as *chemotherapy, anti-nausea medications, blood transfusions,* and *PET scans* quickly became household words.

Paul prayed for the believers in Rome: "Now may the God of hope fill you with all joy and peace in believing, so that you will abound in hope by the power of the Holy Spirit" (Romans 15:13 NASB). Hope is a reservoir of emotional strength, and without it, we sink into self-pity. If we don't consistently preach hope in God to ourselves, then we will find ourselves with a discouraged and unsettled spirit. Through the Holy Spirit, God provides the strength that we need to deal with the troubles of today. But more importantly, He provides us with hope for tomorrow. Because of our faith in the finished work of Jesus Christ on the cross, we can be confident of a future in heaven, where we will spend eternity praising God and enjoying the gift of being reunited with fellow believers who have gone before us.

At 2:51 p.m. on April 28, 2016, Brooklyn witnessed her dad's last breath on this earth. Imagine what occurred in that moment for him. This was his moment of glorification; his faith was made sight. He was immediately free from pain, excess fluid, and cancerous tumors. At that moment, he was personally united with the Son of God Who was slain for us.

Look at God through your circumstances, and He will seem very distant and small. But if through faith you look at your circumstances through God, He will draw very near and reveal His greatness to you. At Brooklyn's university, God brought together four girls who lost their dads on April 28th—different years, but all on that date. God has used that group of girls to minister grace to each other's hearts.

Brooklyn and I have two precious treasures to remind us of Tim's triumph: a t-shirt quilt assembled for Brooklyn by dear friends and a gratitude journal that we kept during his sickness. Our hearts are refreshed reading back through the entries of God's faithfulness through what Tim referred to as his "cancer assignment." Record those acts of His faithfulness in your life. Because, when you look back and re-read what He has done and what He has brought you through, it will give you peace. You will see how His sovereign hand and perfect plan carried you through.

Let the hope of the gospel stir your heart to trust Him with your next steps.

—TRACEE

A Mother's Shame

READ HEBREWS 12:3–17

"A child left to himself brings shame to his mother." PROVERBS 29:15

One of the memorable lines from Charles Dickens' classic novel *Great Expectations* is about how Pip's older sister "brought him up by hand"—Dickens' way of describing discipline. Sadly, we live in a world in which children are abused, much like many of the pitiful children in Dickens' novels—from Oliver Twist to Smike. However, rejection of sinful beatings mustn't be expanded to rejection of biblical discipline. The Bible certainly doesn't justify wonton abuse, despite those who have hijacked Scripture even as they've bullied their children. But the Bible does teach—indeed, *require*—loving discipline.

Biblical discipline is always motivated by love. Scripture teaches that those who love their children will demonstrate it through discipline, when necessary. Indeed, it gives God as the ultimate example of loving discipline for His children's good (Proverb 3:11–12; Hebrews 12:4–11). I once heard a Christian mother explain that she loved her daughter too much to discipline her. But Proverbs 13:24 says the opposite is true: Lack of discipline is an act of *hatred*, whereas discipline shows love.

Biblical discipline is instructive, not merely punitive. I think it's important to differentiate between discipline and punishment. Punishment focuses primarily on retribution for a wrong action. Discipline can build on this, but it is much more. Discipline focuses on transformation. Discipline is discipleship. It teaches your child that "crime doesn't pay." It motivates righteousness. In the words of Proverbs 22:15, it drives folly from him. As Proverbs 23:13–14 says, it may "save his soul from Sheol"—the ultimate punishment. Like an inoculation, it gives a small and short-term discomfort in order to give long-term protection. The implications of this are many. You don't discipline merely to render "justice." You don't discipline out of anger—ever. You discipline in a way that brings about instruction from Scripture—preferably ending with a hug, a prayer, and a smile.

Biblical discipline is consistent. Your child shouldn't be surprised by discipline. Proverbs 13:24 calls for discipline that is "diligent." Arbitrary discipline is worse than no discipline. Your children shouldn't be in bigger trouble because you've had a bad day, or you've had an argument with their dad, or you're just tired. Your discipline should start with a clear warning, perhaps with a single reminder, then be carried out without a lot of angst. The truth is, the reason you yell at your kids is often because you haven't disciplined them, but let things escalate to the point where you're both at wit's end. Don't tolerate bad behavior for a long period, then suddenly snap. Be consistent. That means you must discipline yourself. Jim Berg has wisely said, "The problem isn't strong-willed kids. It's weak-willed parents."

Biblical discipline is temporary. This is extremely important. Your goal is to discipline your child so consistently at a young age that you can start weaning them off as they progress toward adolescence. The equation of Proverbs 29:17 is *discipline now = delight later*. In other words, if you'll do a really good job when they're toddlers, the teen years can be a joy, not a gauntlet. By God's grace, that's been our experience. We were parents to our girls as children, and we've enjoyed being friends and counselors to our girls as teenagers. Bishop J. C. Ryle taught this point brilliantly: "A boy may bend an oak, when it is a sapling—a hundred men cannot root it up, when it is a full-grown tree."

Discipline. Don't just punish. Certainly don't injure. Give loving discipline, followed by a loving hug. You'll save your child—and yourself—a lot of grief in the long run. Let the gospel help you discipline your kids like our Father disciplines His.—CHRIS

Daily Devotions for Moms

READ MATTHEW 6

"Ask, and it shall be given to you; seek, and you will find." MATTHEW 7:7

How are your devotions going? Many Christians hear the word *devotions* and immediately feel guilty because they compare so unfavorably to some heroic Christian who devoted several hours a day to Bible reading and prayer. A busy mom hears the word and thinks, "Impossible!" because, from morning to night, her only "quiet time" is when she locks the door for a minute in the bathroom—and sometimes even that moment is bombarded with screaming in the hallway and banging on the door. You might be surprised to discover that, in the chapter of the Bible that most directly focuses on a disciple's acts of devotion, what Jesus demands isn't some unattainable time spent in quiet, but a devoted focus on the gospel in all your daily activities.

Daily prayer for gospel advance expresses your heart's devotion (vv. 1–18). Jesus is burdened that you practice your acts of devotion sincerely, not so that others will take notice and think highly of you (v. 1). He is particularly concerned that you pray every day for the advance of God's agenda (vv. 5–15). And lest you think that your daily prayers should be hours long and of publishable quality, Jesus suggested that your daily habit be six simple sentences, prayed sincerely not mindlessly. He commands you to pray first for God's name to be glorified, for His kingdom to be established on earth, and for His will to be obeyed. Until Jesus returns to reign, God is glorified especially as sinners respond to the gospel with saving faith. After you pray for God's agenda to advance, Jesus then commands you to pray for your daily provisions, for forgiveness of recent sins, and for strength to resist temptation. Such simple prayer at the start of every day expresses your devotion to the gospel's advance around you and within you.

Daily investment in gospel advance shows your heart's devotion (vv. 19–24). Jesus teaches that your investments reveal the devotion of your heart. He bluntly observes that your heart is devoted either to "treasures on earth" or to "treasures in heaven," but never to both. You "lay up . . . treasures on earth" when you spend your time and money on things that won't last. You "lay up . . . treasures in heaven" when you invest your time and money on things that will last—namely, people. You invest in eternity as you evangelize and disciple your children and as you support the members and ministry of your gospel-preaching church. Your investments in the gospel's advance are acts of devotion.

Daily "worry" over gospel advance reveals your heart's devotion (vv. 25–34). Jesus urges you to "seek first" (that is, be primarily devoted to) God's kingdom. He warns you not to worry about your daily needs such as food and clothing because God will take care of such things. Of course, Jesus is not saying that you as a mother should avoid budgeting and shopping for groceries and clothing (see Proverbs 31:14–22). Nor, when He promises that "all these things will be added to you" (v. 33), is Jesus guaranteeing that you will never lack daily necessities. Instead, Jesus is teaching about worry. He's saying in essence, "Worry about the gospel's advance, trusting that your Father will take care of your needs according to His good plan for you." And, to exterminate your worries, Jesus tells you to stop and consider the purpose of life (v. 25), consider the birds and flowers and your comparative value (vv. 26–30), consider the futility of worry (v. 27), consider the present state of your trust in God (v. 30), and consider how much your caring Father knows about you and your situation (v. 32). Such considerations should shift your focus away from temporary concerns and lead you to a preoccupation with the gospel—an act of daily devotion.

Let the gospel be central in your daily acts of devotion.—JOE

Love That Endures

READ PSALM 136
"His steadfast love endures forever." PSALM 136:1

One of the great things about being a pastor's wife is that I usually get a preview of what's coming on Sunday morning. One of the bad things about being a pastor's wife is that it can sometimes be difficult to really hear the Word of God proclaimed. While everyone else has a certain amount of distance from the man behind the pulpit, I see my husband. I see the man whose laundry I wash and meals I cook. I see the man I have lived with day in and day out for the last sixteen years. But one Sunday, while my husband was preaching from Psalm 136, I heard the Scripture more loudly than was comfortable.

This psalm recounts God's glory by retelling how He had worked in Israel's history; from creating the heavens and the "great lights" to dividing the Red Sea to bringing Israel into the Promised Land and defeating their enemies. Each of the twenty-six verses repeats the phrase "for his steadfast love endures forever."

As my husband was unfolding the truth of God's enduring faithfulness, the Holy Spirit pricked my conscience: *Daughter, how often do you endure? How often do you expect steadfast love to come easily? How often do you give up too soon—especially when it comes to your children?*

Being the good Christian that I am, my defenses went up immediately. "But you don't understand," I fought back. "You're God; mercy and faithfulness come naturally to you. And my children? Well, they're so foolish—and messy and disorganized and lazy. I have to yell at them or they won't get the point. I have to become exasperated or they just keep doing what they're doing."

Yes, they are foolish. But do you endure?

"Oh, you have no idea how much I endure."

No, do you push past the barrier of your frustration? Do you let your love soften your anger? Do you endure? Like I do?

I knew, of course, that I didn't. That too often I confused childishness with disobedience. That I too quickly embraced my "righteous anger." That I needed to repent.

We often imagine God as a fixed character in a cosmic drama—He is the Constant to our development, the Foil to our inconstancy. And while it's true that He never changes, we must not confuse His active faithfulness with being flat or static. He is no cardboard cut-out. He is not a force or concept or paradigm. He is the *living* God. He exists in a kaleidoscope of love and justice, and mercy and holiness, with nothing but His own divine power holding the tension together. So when David says that God's mercy endures forever, perhaps it does just that: It *endures*.

It endures our foolishness; it endures our stubbornness; it endures our weakness. Like a long-distance runner, it pushes on to the finish line of our salvation, long past the point where mere mortals give up. So that with lungs bursting and sweat dripping, His longsuffering becomes true suffering, and through Christ, His mercy willfully and strongly holds back His divine and justified wrath.

Shakespeare writes that mercy falls "like the gentle rain from heaven." And to us at least, it feels like rain, like cool, calming, life-giving rain on our parched souls. But we must not think that what comes down to us so easily has been won easily. The mercy we receive from God was hard-won through the struggle of His Son on the cross. Mercy does not simply fall. Mercy fights and endures.

Let the gospel humble you when you remember how much God's mercy has endured on your behalf.—HANNAH

A Dash of Critique,
A Dump Truck of Commendation

READ 1 CORINTHIANS 1:1-9; PHILIPPIANS 1:1-5; AND 1 THESSALONIANS 1:1-10

"Gracious words are like a honeycomb, sweetness to the soul and health to the body."
PROVERBS 16:24

My family has a tradition which I think you should adopt. Every time someone has a birthday—*every* time!—we give that person the gift of compliments. Yes, we have cake, and ice cream, and presents. But at some point during our celebration, we take turns telling the person things we genuinely admire about her. Inevitably one of my girls will pretend to be stumped, like she just can't think of *anything* positive to say about her sister. But after that predictable joke, we share a precious time together. It's embarrassing to the birthday girl. But it's also deeply encouraging.

You work so hard, even when you're tired. . . . You are so genuinely kind and unselfish, even when I'm being difficult. . . . I love your smile; it encourages me! . . . You aren't affected by peer pressure; I admire that so much!

Now, I'm not suggesting that we raise our children in a millennial, post-modern, politically-correct "safe space." Your children need your correction. They need you to say, "no." They need you to support the teacher rather than undermining the teacher and taking up for your precious and perfect eight-year-old. (Note to self: The teacher is always right. Always.) Part of loving your child is disciplining him and confronting him when he sins.

But for every dash of criticism, unload a dump truck of praise.

Some of you will have to work at it, just like some of you will have to work at the correction side. But affirmation is vital, especially if you're prone to over-critique. Parents who are hardwired to see only faults—or even many faults—do far more harm than they realize:

Thanks for making dessert, honey, but it would have been better if . . . . You look really nice today, but what's up with your hair? . . . It was nice of you to do the laundry, but next time. . . . Nice goal today, son, but you could have had three.

Critiques like that are like a dripping faucet. They erode your child's confidence—and no, I'm not doing an Oprah impersonation—It matters! Worse, they erode your relationship with your child. Constant criticism is exasperating and repulsive. Soon they'll stop listening to you altogether.

I'm grateful for the example of Paul, who opened letters to even the worst of churches by thanking God for them. Yes, he often gave more than a "dash" of correction. But he was always very expressive of (a) things he admired and thanked God for in their lives, and (b) how deeply he loved them.

An even better example is our Lord Jesus. When inspecting the seven churches in Revelation 2–3, He repeatedly commended them wherever He could: "I know your works."

Your children live in a world that will gladly reprimand them. They'll get a lifetime of reproof. Sure, you should teach them how to take it. But you certainly want to err on the side of grace. Look for evidences of virtues, not just vices, whether your children are toddlers or teens. Practice positive reinforcement: Praise the things you want to encourage. When you see something admirable, tell them so! Be their biggest cheerleader! You don't even have to wait for a birthday.

Let the gospel make you a genuinely gracious and positive parent.—CHRIS

The Source of Your Strength

READ ISAIAH 30:1–22 AND 35:1–10

"In quietness and in trust shall be your strength." ISAIAH 30:15

Mothers are in desperate need of strength—both physical and spiritual. But where does strength come from? It's ironic and instructive that much of our *physical* stamina comes from doing absolutely nothing—that is, from sleeping. (Which helps to explain why many moms are so physically weary.) Where does *spiritual* strength come from? Let's explore the heart of Isaiah's prophecy to find the answer.

How familiar are you with Isaiah 28–35? Probably not very. These eight chapters have to rank among the least known chapters in the Bible. They're in the middle of one of the longest books of the most unpopular sections of the Bible—the Old Testament prophets. More, these chapters predominantly focus on the unpopular subject of judgment for sin. (See Isaiah's repeated exclamations of grief—"Ah!"— over the misery that's ahead for Israel [28:1; 29:1, 15; 30:1; 31:1; 33:1].) But these chapters are invaluable for us today, not only because judgment still looms over everyone who ignores God's authority, and not only because Jesus and His apostles continually quoted from them (see, for example, Matthew 15:8; 1 Corinthians 1:19; Hebrews 12:12; James 3:18; and 1 Peter 2:6), but especially because Isaiah reveals the path from judgment to hope—from spiritual shambles to spiritual strength.

God's goal in pronouncing judgment is always to produce a response of repentance—to decisively turn people away from their rebellion. Throughout these chapters, the Lord urges people in Israel to turn away from seeking security in their military alliance with Egypt and to rely only on Him. Notice the Lord's counsel in Isaiah 30:15: "In returning and rest you shall be saved; in quietness and in trust shall be your strength." The way to security and peace is repentance and faith. Isn't that contrary to the way we think? We typically assume that strength comes through lots of work. But that's not how *spiritual* strength comes. Gideon didn't need to add more soldiers but to expel the cowards. David slew Goliath only after he shed Saul's armor. Hezekiah conquered the massive Assyrian army not with a clever military alliance but by "spread[ing his crisis] before the Lord" (Isaiah 37:14). Spiritual strength comes by trusting the Lord, not redoubling your efforts!

As you read this devotional, it may be that you are like Israel—far down the road of distrust. You've heaped sin on sin (30:1). What do you suppose to be God's attitude toward you? Isaiah assures you that "the LORD waits to be gracious to you, and therefore he exalts himself to show mercy to you. For the LORD is a God of justice; blessed are all those who wait for him" (30:18). The God of justice wants to show you kindness. Incredible! The God of justice actually took on Himself the punishment for your rebellion so that He can offer you forgiveness if you'll turn and entrust your life to Him. The God who bore your sin isn't merely *able* to be gracious; He is *wanting* to be gracious to you (30:18–19).

Trusting God isn't a once-and-done thing. Isaiah goes on to describe a glorious future for God's people—a reality for which God-trusters must continually hope (30:19–22; see also 35:4–10). One day, the Lord will return to earth and rid the world of all sickness, all sin, all strife, all sorrow, and all sighing. The proof that this glorious day will come was guaranteed when Jesus, in His first coming, healed diseases, calmed storms, and raised the dead. If you have trusted Jesus, you're following the One took all your sorrows on Himself at His first coming and who will rid you of all sorrows (and exchange them for joy) at His second coming. Such glorious hope "strengthen[s] weak hands" (35:3).

Let the God of the gospel be your primary Source of day-to-day strength.—JOE

Sleep Like a Calvinist

READ PSALM 127

"He gives to his beloved sleep." PSALM 127:2

....

Moms worry. White knuckling is part of the job description. They worry about their child's safety, health, character, and future. It's normal. But excessive worry can be a "check engine light," revealing some wrong thinking, and even some bad theology. Psalm 127:1–2 address a mother's anxiety with instruction, and even a bit of gentle reproof.

Excessive worry shows that you're overestimating your role in training your child. There are mothers who are disengaged and passive. But in my experience, they're the exception. Most mothers are very attentive to the needs of their children. The trouble is, attention can easily turn to obsession. The whole point of Psalm 127:1 is that your efforts, though necessary, are insufficient. Your children need your "building" (the first picture of the verse) and "protecting" (the second picture of the verse). The point is, they need *more*. They need *the Lord* to build them up and protect them, in addition to the work of their parents. Otherwise their parents work is "in vain." Psalm 127:2 gets even more pointed: Your stressed-out busyness—rising early and staying up late, and worrying all the while ("eating the bread of anxious toil")—is also "vain." Scripture isn't arguing against industry and diligence. It's arguing against the mindset that your child's physical safety and spiritual health are all dependent on you. Your anxiety probably reveals that you're thinking more highly of your influence than you ought to. Yes, you're part of the parenting equation. An important part! But you're not all of it.

Excessive worry shows that you're underestimating God's role in training your child. The focus of Psalm 127:1–2 isn't merely on the inadequacy of the parent's effort. Instead, it's on the blessing of God's infinitely superior effort. God is more than able to "build" your house. God is more than able to "watch" and protect your family. He uses you in the process. But thankfully, He's not limited by your limitations. This is great news! God is able to do for your children what you cannot! Raising children who know and love God is above your pay grade; it's not above His!

Excessive worry shows that you're doubting God's goodness. Anxiety doesn't reveal just that you're doubting God *can* take care of your children better than you can. It shows that you're doubting if He even *wants to*. The essence of worry is a denial of God's goodness. I've heard someone put it this candidly: "I know God is all-powerful. I'm just not sure that He likes me very much." I've had that feeling more than once. But it's rubbish! God isn't just omnipotent. He's omni-benevolent. He's omni-compassionate. He's omni-gracious. The bottom line is this, mom: God can't only take better care of your children than you can—God *loves* your children more than you do! You can trust Him.

Excessive worry is robbing you of God's gracious gift of rest. I love the last line of Psalm 127:2: "He gives to his beloved sleep." It's such a contrast from the dawn-to-dusk fretting of the first part of the verse. The idea is simply this: Work hard, then rest (physically and emotionally), knowing that God has everything under control. I tell people to "sleep like a Calvinist." Even if you'd not self-identify as a Calvinist in your theology, the idea is that you enjoy the ease and peace that comes from the belief that an all-good, all-wise God is managing the lives of your children just as He manages the sun, moon, and stars. God is in charge. You're not, nor do you need to be. Nor do you *want* to be! Obey the Scriptures as best you can, by His grace. Tuck in your kids. Breathe out a prayer of thanks and faith. Then *rest*.

Let the gospel help you to stop fretting as though you were sovereign and start resting as though God is!—CHRIS

Learn from the Queen of Sheba

READ 1 KINGS 10:1–13

"And King Solomon gave to the queen of Sheba all that she desired." 1 KINGS 10:13

The queen of Sheba's trip to Jerusalem to visit King Solomon is the last glorious glimpse we get of the great King Solomon in Scripture. As a foreign woman, this queen stands out in Old Testament history like Rahab and Ruth because, even though she didn't grow up in Israel, she comes to recognize something of the glory of Israel's God. She recognizes that Israel's king is wise because of God's blessing and that the whole nation is blessed as a result. And she really gets our hopes up that maybe the historic promises that God made to Abraham (a millennium before) and David (a generation before) might finally come to fulfillment—that the rulers on earth will submit themselves to Israel's glorious God and king. This passage is all about the increasing international fame of Israel's God-chosen, God-blessed king.

How does this ancient encounter pertain to you? One verse in the New Testament, Matthew 12:42, unlocks the application of 1 Kings 10 for Christians today. There Jesus tells His listeners that this queen "will rise up at the judgment with [the generation in Israel that rejected Jesus] and condemn it, for she came from the ends of the earth to hear the wisdom of Solomon, and behold, something greater than Solomon is here." In other words, on judgment day this queen is going to be brought forward as a witness against those who rejected Jesus. She's going to stand in God's courtroom and say something like this: "I traveled fifteen hundred miles on camelback to visit Solomon. These people in Jesus' day didn't have to travel a lick. *He came to them!* He was much wiser than Solomon, and yet they were thoroughly unimpressed." See, wise King Solomon foreshadows Israel's much greater and much wiser King, Jesus (who came from Solomon's line a millennium later). Unlike Solomon, Jesus obeyed God perfectly. Unlike Solomon, the peace that Jesus brings won't be limited to one country for less than a generation; it will be worldwide and eternal. Unlike Solomon, Jesus won't be praised by a handful of dignitaries; He'll be honored by "every tongue," including countless rescued sinners from "every tribe and language and people and nation" (Philippians 2:11; Revelation 5:9).

So, if you're wise like this foreign queen, you'll explore for yourself the reports of Israel's wisest King (vv. 1–5), and you'll praise Jesus as the Source of wisdom, Giver of joy, and King of justice (vv. 7–9). And, if you're wise like this ancient queen, you'll offer your gifts to Israel's wisest King (v. 10).

The queen offered Solomon gifts of gold and spices from her country. From her perspective, the gifts were generous. From Solomon's perspective, they weren't all that significant. (Solomon's annual income of gold was five times greater than what this queen gave him on this occasion.) Yet the gifts were meaningful because they conveyed honor on the king. Are you a mom who beats yourself up for everything you try to give your King. In your eyes, are your gifts meager? At the end of the day, is your common self-assessment that the Lord must be dissatisfied with a failure like you? If that's you, then notice how this passage ends. After the queen gave what she could, the king gave to her "from his bounty"—He gave her "anything she asked for" (v. 13). What a foreshadowing of King Jesus who came to give "from his full-ness . . . grace upon grace" (John 1:16)! Mom, when you flop in bed and prayerfully bring all your unimpressive efforts of the day to King Jesus, saying, "Here it is Jesus: today's efforts at motherhood," what are you going to get from Him? Is the King going to chide you for not giving more? No, you're going to get grace—lavish grace from His bounty—all the grace you need, all the grace you desire.

Let the lavish grace of the gospel encourage you to keep honoring the King with your seemingly feeble efforts.—JOE

Tennis Shoes, Rice Krispies Treats, and Tears

READ ROMANS 12

"Rejoice with those who rejoice, weep with those who weep." ROMANS 12:15

I have the best mom in the world. Actually, she's tied with the mother of my four daughters. Sorry, but the rest of you are vying for third place. What makes my mother so wonderful? So much. The impossibly generous lunches she packed that made me the envy of my friends. The pantry that she filled with a scandalous amount of junk food. The old dresses she wore and wore and wore for a good decade so her three boys had nice school clothes and name-brand tennis shoes. She spoiled us, I guess, though not by winking at poor behavior. She was indulgent, but not permissive. (Mercy, the woman turned into a ninja when it was time to wield her wooden spoon.) But she put us first, all the time.

She made me love music. She has an amazing touch on the piano, even now when her fingers are being gnarled by arthritis. And she loves to harmonize—she has a strong alto voice and a great ear, both of which my daughter Esther inherited. The fact that I have memorized a library-full of hymns, gospel songs, and "Favorites" from the old John W. Peterson books (with their amazingly tight harmonies) is my mom's fault. (Thank you, Mom!)

Mom taught me to love writing. Even today she's still my best editor, often emailing me a list of typos or grammatical errors we missed in our multiple edits of the *Gospel Meditations* books. I have two "mom memories" from my elementary years that propelled me toward my obsession with writing today. First, my poor mother would give in to my incessant requests to play "The Rhyme Game" every time we were in the car together. I'd give a word, and she'd have to come up with a rhyme. Back and forth we'd go until one of us was stumped. (I still do the same mental gymnastics forty years later, working my way through the alphabet: "A: ACE. B: Bace. BASS! Blace. BRACE! C: CASE!" And so on.) If my hymns rhyme today, it's Mom's fault! I also remember her taking my dictations on a couple of third grade reports after I'd broken my right arm (for the third time). One report was on golden eagles, and the other on hammerhead sharks. I told her what to write, and she obediently filled the page with her beautiful cursive, capturing my words as carefully as if I were writing the Declaration of Independence.

There are countless other memories. Mom cheering at all my ballgames. Mom learning to love sports so she could talk to her sports-crazed boys. Mom sending newspaper articles about my Denver Broncos to me every week during college (before the internet), along with her famous Rice Krispies Treats and applesauce (which she'd freeze first so it would still be cold when it arrived days later).

My most vivid memory, though, is about a girl. I was dating someone in high school, and Mom wasn't excited about it. After about a year of dating, we broke up. I am certain that Mom was inwardly rejoicing. I arrived home from school after seeing the girl with another guy, and I was utterly disconsolate. I'd managed to keep my emotions in check all day, but seeing Mom—and trying to tell her—made me melt. I wept as though my world were ending. Mom hugged me. She didn't lecture me or gloat. I kept crying, and she finally started to sob herself. I was shocked. She was relieved that the relationship was over, but her chest heaved even more than mine. She made my pain hers. She bore it with me. And I'll never forget it.

Mom said wise things to me, to be sure. She gave me plenty of spankings when I needed them. But what I remember most—and what your children will remember most in a few decades—is a mother's lavish love expressed in big ways and small.

Let the gospel help you love your children as unconditionally as your Heavenly Father loves you.—CHRIS

Trust God's Plans for Your Child

READ PSALM 46

"God is our refuge and strength, a very present help in trouble." PSALM 46:1

My knees grew weak as I heard the neurosurgeon say, "Dr. Sood and I have reviewed your daughter's case, and our recommendation is surgery to excise the cyst." I numbly stood in an aisle at Target as I hung up the phone. A stealth-guided occipital transtentorial resection brain surgery would soon be performed on my sixteen-year-old daughter.

Eight months of constant head pain and pressure led to an MRI, which resulted in the discovery of the grape-sized cyst on the pineal gland in the center of Brooklyn's head. Two neurosurgeons performed a five-hour surgery. Initially, she teased her dad by pretending not to recognize him; she always had his sense of humor. But that long first night in ICU was agonizing. Sensing her discomfort and wondering what her head actually looked like under the layers of bandages made for an excruciating night of anxiety in this mom's heart.

"When my anxious thoughts multiply within me, Your consolations delight my soul" (Psalm 94:19 NASB). Somehow this verse—one that had previously gone unnoticed by me—became my anchor through bleak days when no amount of snuggling, medication, or dark rooms could alleviate Brooklyn's pain. Naturally, I had pleaded for God to remove the pain, or at least for the pain to be transferred from her head to mine. That was not His sovereign plan for her, and although the surgery was absolutely necessary and was considered successful, the cyst had nothing to do with her head pain.

Watching your child endure chronic pain is heart-wrenching. And yet, we have a loving Father who watched His own dear Son as He was brutally crucified. Because Jesus was abandoned on the cross, we never will be—not in the hospital waiting room, not in the ICU, not even in a dark basement with months of recovery. Knowing that God would never abandon us was a huge consolation to our hurting hearts.

When God's sovereign plan includes something you never would have chosen for your child, don't fret over trying to understand His ways. Simply trust that while we may only see a few threads, God sees the entire tapestry. To this day my daughter's head pain continues. God has chosen not to remove it. Do I believe He could relinquish her pain? Absolutely. What He has chosen to do instead is to shape my daughter's heart and faith as she leans on Him for her daily strength. He has given her a heart of empathy towards others in long-term struggles. And He has knit her heart and mine together.

Six weeks after the craniotomy, we realized that she couldn't fully heal while staying in school. Brooklyn stayed home for the remainder of the school year, which led to her high school graduation being postponed by a year. What a difficult thing for a sixteen-year-old to grasp. But unbeknownst to us, God was graciously paving the way for what lay ahead for our family (see Day 11). He's good. He's sovereign. And He's continuing to carry her through this trial. His grace is sufficent for her—and for me, the mother who has to watch her suffer (2 Corinthians 12:9). This portion of a poem Brooklyn penned on October 22, 2013 reminds me of God's gracious design:

> During the storm, we may not understand.
> But it's all intertwined in His purpose and plan.

Let the gospel console your anxious heart as you trust God's perfect plans for your child.—TRACEE

Adorable Little Pagans

READ PSALM 51

"Behold, I was brought forth in iniquity, and in sin did my mother conceive me." PSALM 51:5

One of my joys as a pastor is participating in people's most memorable moments, including weddings, funerals, and baptisms. A special joy is the baby dedication. Per my understanding of Scripture (and with apologies to my Presbyterian friends), it's not a baptism. But it's a precious time to give thanks to God for entrusting this young child to her parents. It's a time to charge them to labor and pray toward that child's salvation, and to charge our church family to labor alongside with them to that same end. It's a time to pray that God will draw the child to Himself—so that after she is born again by faith in Christ, we can baptize her! During these sweet times, I almost always use the same joke. I congratulate the parents on the birth of their "adorable little pagan." People kindly laugh, though it's more at my predictability than my delivery. But it's not a wasted comment. There's a lesson in it.

First, your child came into the world as a sinner. She's a pagan. That may surprise first-time parents, but they'll learn soon enough. Experience will teach them that their daughter didn't need to learn to be selfish, to defiantly disobey them, or to throw tantrums. They're naturals. More than experience, Scripture teaches this. Children are born sinners. They aren't sinners as a result of sinning. They sin as a result of being sinners. David said as much in Psalm 51:5. He wasn't lamenting some sin on the part of his mother, as though she had been an adulteress. He is confessing that from the moment of his conception he was a sinner. All of us are born in sin, inherited from Adam (Romans 5:12). We are sinners both by birth and by choice. Your cherubic little baby is a rebel against God.

Second, your child needs to be born again. The hope for your little rebel isn't learning good manners or first-time obedience. Her hope—her *only* hope—is having her sins washed away through the blood of Jesus. Your first and most important responsibility as a parent is to teach your child the gospel. Yes, you need to teach her other things, including obedience and kindness. But those lessons won't save her soul. You must teach her the gospel, as early and as often as possible. Timothy's mom did this (2 Timothy 1:5; 3:15). From infancy, the adorable little pagan named Timmy was learning the Scriptures which would eventually save him. Follow Eunice's example. Teach your child about sin, about God's love, about Jesus' substitutionary death. Don't water it down to "asking Jesus into her heart." Make sure she knows exactly what Jesus did, and why. And as you teach it, pray. Ask God to draw your daughter to Himself in salvation, knowing that you are unable to do His great wooing work (John 6:44).

Third, your child will live somewhere forever. It's sobering to consider that your cooing, drooling baby girl will live somewhere forever: hell or heaven; eternal death or eternal life (Romans 6:23). There's no third option. There's no opting out. Her life began at conception, but it will never end. *Never.* You're not raising her to be a good toddler, or a polite teen, or a successful adult. Your ultimate goal is to shepherd her toward eternity, knowing that if she gains the whole world but loses her own soul, it will be an infinitely bad bargain.

Parenting is serious business. Eternity hangs in the balance. Enjoy your beautiful baby. Smile and laugh and photograph and scrapbook. But never forget that she's a pagan. She needs the Savior. Teach her that, then pray for God to do for her what you cannot. And look forward to rejoicing together in your mutual salvation when He does—both now and for eternity.

Let the gospel be the most important lesson you pass on to your child.—CHRIS

Every Good and Perfect Gift

READ JAMES 1:1–18

"Every good gift and every perfect gift is from above." JAMES 1:17

Jesus' half-brother James penned a letter to Christians who were experiencing severe trials and who, in their difficulties, were tempted to get mad at God—embittered, suspicious, and pessimistic. James urged these weary believers to take time to consider again what God is like. He wrote, "Every good gift and every perfect gift is from above, coming down from the Father of lights with whom there is no variation or shadow due to change" (v. 17). Here's what God is like: He only gives good gifts; He is the mighty Creator of the sun, moon, and stars; He—even more fixed than stars—is unchanging in His pure goodness. This beautifully expressed truth must control a Christian mom's outlook on life—her trials and all!

Your daily attitude should reflect your conviction that God is only and always good. When life is hard, you're tempted to think, "Why did God allow this? I thought He was leading me! I thought He loved me!" You can't interpret God's character based on your circumstances. You must interpret your circumstances by what you know about God: He's good—only and always good. The apostle James says that the brilliant light of God's goodness is brighter, purer, and more constant than the sun. That conviction must undergird your daily attitude.

When you're particularly low and need proof of God's goodness, look at yourself. James says that one of the best examples of God's goodness is that He chose to save us (v. 18). Need proof that God is good? He gave a sinner like you new life through the message of the gospel. And He wasn't just willing to save you; He *wanted* to save you. That's why He provided His Son to bear the punishment that you justly deserved for your sins, and that's why He worked in your heart to turn you from your condemnable self-centeredness. So, if God desired to save you when you were a rebel, how certain are you, now that you're His child, that everything He allows in your life is only for your good? You are living proof of God's goodness.

What God has given you in your domestic life is a really good gift. Marriage and family, as hard as they can be, are two of the good and perfect gifts that come down to us from God above. Marriage and family are God's inventions, and we're told on the first page of the Bible that marriage is part of His "very good" creation. He created marriage—life-long covenant-keeping love between a man who's a servant-minded leader and a woman who's a servant-minded supporter. And He created all the beautiful things that come with marriage for your good as well—things like friendship, teamwork, romance, sexuality, and the possibility of children.

Every trial you encounter is a good gift from God. If God is God, and if He's only and always good, you can always consider every trial in your life to be God's gift to you for your good (vv. 2–4). This includes every domestic trial that you face, even the abandonment of a spouse or the loss of a child. Because marriage and family come with painful challenges, at times you won't feel like they are good gifts. But you can be certain that every trial God puts in your domestic life is there to strengthen, purify, and mature you. So you can endure with solid joy.

James implores you to remember that God is always and only good, that He saved you because He is so good, that you enjoy many good gifts from God like marriage and family, and that every trial you endure is all for your good. May those who know you sense warm thankfulness and solid joy because James 1:17 is the banner that flies over your life.

Let the gospel of God's goodness fill your daily life with joy and thankfulness.—JOE

Rest for the Weary

READ HEBREWS 4:1–10

"Whoever has entered God's rest has also rested from his works as God did from his." HEBREWS 4:10

The last several weeks have been particularly busy ones, and as a result, I've found myself feeling out of sorts, irritable, and generally put upon. You know what I mean: when every *"Mommy, can you help me . . . "* feels like an obligation; when each new opportunity weighs you down; when you reach the end of your endurance and just want people to leave you alone.

Truthfully, it's my own fault. I am no perfectionist, but I do have a tendency to busyness. I have a hard time saying no, winding down, and truly resting. Over the years, I've had to admit this inability to stop as a weakness and commit to creating quiet space in my life. I've learned that rest is an act of faith, that I can stop working precisely because I believe that God will work for me. But recently I've learned that rest is also an act of self-control.

The first time that the Scripture mentions the concept of rest is in Genesis 2:3 when God rests after creation. He didn't rest because He was tired, but to model rest for us. And part of what He models is His own self-mastery. By abstaining from work, by purposefully limiting His creative power, He shows that He is not mastered by anything. Just because He could have done more didn't mean He had to.

So too for us, rest is not only a form of trust. It's also a way to express the freedom and power that He has given us through the gospel. When we rest and purposefully abstain from work, we declare that we are no longer slaves to our baser selves. We are no longer driven by our fears, desires, or even the demands of those around us. We declare that we are mastered by nothing but Him.

In Matthew 11:28–30 Christ calls those who are weary and heavy laden to come to Him for rest. But He provides this rest in an unexpected way: by calling us to come under His control. "Take my yoke upon you," He invites, "and learn from me, for I am gentle and lowly in heart. . . . My yoke is easy, and my burden is light."

Christ's call to rest is a call to come away from other masters and submit to Him alone. It is a call to come away from following the expectations of other people and our own sense of performance. It is a call to be conformed to nothing but His perfect image, to allow His nature to mold and shape our own. So that as we follow Him, our souls—just like His—will be free from the weight, free from the strain, free from the feeling of being driven like a pack-animal. "For God has not given us a spirit of fear," Paul reminds us in 2 Timothy 1:7, "but of power and love and self-control."

When feelings of bitterness and discouragement creep up inside you, do not simply push them aside and soldier on. Instead take the opportunity to evaluate whether you have enslaved yourself to something other than Christ. Take the opportunity to remember that He is a good, kind Master whose yoke is easy and burden is light.

God commands us to rest in Exodus 20:8–11 because He knows how desperately we need it—physically, spiritually, mentally, and emotionally. Stop trying to impress others, yourself, and even God with your self-inflicted busyness. Learn the joy of rest.

Let the gospel free you to rest.—HANNAH

Blessed in Crisis

READ PSALM 84

"O Lord of hosts, blessed is the one who trusts in you!" PSALM 84:12

....

If you are in a life-sapping crisis, and you're looking for a break, look at Psalm 84. The song's final line reveals that it's overall tone is *delight*, which is remarkable because it's delight in the middle of crisis. Israel's king was in trouble (vv. 8–9). No one knows exactly what crisis the king was in: maybe he was under threat, was making horrible choices, or had been deported. We don't know. But what's certain is that this psalm was written in a time of personal crisis. How striking then that the song is saturated with delight—with the psalmist's sense of privilege (vv. 4, 5, 12). The song presents three reasons to rejoice during crisis.

You are blessed with a lovely home (vv. 1–4). The psalmist is longing—even, fainting!—to be where the Lord is. He's encouraged by the sparrows and swallows that nest in the temple. Jim Boice helpfully points out that these two birds are known for their near worthlessness and frequent restlessness (*Psalms*, pp. 690–91; see Proverbs 26:2 and Luke 12:6–7). It's like the songwriter is saying, "Lord, these birds give me hope that wherever You are can be home for a restless, undeserving sinner like me." Of course, those today who trust in the Lord experience His presence, not at the temple in Jerusalem, but through personal faith in Jesus (John 2:19; 4:20–24; Matthew 27:51; Hebrews 10:19–22), through regularly gathering with Jesus' church (Matthew 18:20; 2 Corinthians 3:16–17; Ephesians 2:22; 1 Peter 2:5), and through death, because "to be absent from the body [is] to be present with the Lord" (2 Corinthians 5:8 KJV). If you trust the Lord, you can joyfully long for your home with Christ—something no trial can ever take away.

You are blessed with strong help in hardships (vv. 5–8). In the second stanza you are assured that God will bless you in the valley of difficulty—that He will flood your dry valley with rain. In other words, the Lord will transform your seasons of hardship into the most fruitful seasons of your life. If you today are walking through the valley of tears, rejoice that one day soon you'll look back on this time with thanks, saying something like this: "God, in that valley Your grace was abundant. You taught me much. You kept me from losing my faith. You made me stronger. You brought me out. God, I'd never want to go back to that valley, but I wouldn't trade the experience." If you've run to the Lord for refuge, you're blessed to have His strong help through hardship.

You are blessed with happiness in your service (vv. 9–12). Consider with the psalmist what a privilege it is to serve the Lord. Say to God: "No matter how You answer my prayer in the present circumstance, I just want to tell You that there's no pleasure in life better than knowing and serving You. If I had to choose between being a custodian who lives in hardship with You and being a CEO who lives in ease without You, Lord, every time I'd choose to be the custodian!" Those who trust the Lord live with this deep sense of privilege because the Lord, like the sun, gives life and joy and guidance, and like a shield He provides protection and peace. Even more, He gives His children only what is good—something of which you, living on this side of Calvary, are doubly certain (Romans 8:32).

No matter how tough your trial, knowing and serving God is an infinite fountain of delight. Yet such blessings are only for those who trust the Lord—those who have taken refuge in Jesus for forgiveness of sin. If you have embraced Jesus as Lord, you have a lovely home for which you groan, a strong help in hardship, and contented happiness in your service.

Let the gospel flood you with a sense of rich blessing in your time of crisis.—JOE

Strength to Admit Weakness

READ 1 CORINTHIANS 12:1–10

"I can do all things through him who strengthens me." PHILIPPIANS 4:13

It was three days after my second daughter was born. My husband hadn't felt well and finally decided to go to the doctor. He called me with the diagnosis: Influenza B. Because of the newborn in our home and two other young children, the doctor recommended he go into quarantine until he was symptom-free for twenty-four hours.

Standing in our hallway, hearing my husband would not be able to interact or help with the kids for at least five days, my already unstable hormones went into overdrive. Tears ran down my cheeks as I thought of everything I needed help with, how tired I already was, and how I was going to explain Dad's absence to our kids. My limitations quickly became obvious, and the fact that I wasn't strong enough to handle it all was painfully clear. I carried my baby into the bedroom and collapsed in a chair.

It's not easy for moms to admit weakness. We are seen as the guardians of our homes, the influencers of our children, the glue that holds our families together. But sometimes we can't be everything we think we should be for the simple reason that we are human. We are limited in what we can do and what we can control.

The apostle Paul spoke of his weakness beautifully in 1 Corinthians 12. He mentioned a thorn in the flesh that God had given him and not taken away, even after Paul pleaded multiple times to be relieved. Instead God answered, "My grace is sufficient for you, for my power is made perfect in weakness" (v. 9).

What is that power? The same power that raised Christ from the dead! The same power that came down at Pentecost and filled the believers. The statement in Philippians 4:13 is not just wishful thinking. Through Christ and His sacrifice for us, we have strength to do what we have been called to do.

But this strength is not about being self-sufficient and doing it all on our own. It's a strength that comes from realizing we need God, not just in the big decisions or crisis moments, but every day. As we raise our children and interact with others, it becomes clear that we need help. But that help only comes through the weakness that forces us to rely on the gospel and seek God's strength. That's why Paul chose to *boast* in his weakness for the glory of God rather than try to muscle through on his own. That's why he could confidently declare, "When I am weak, then I am strong" (v. 10).

As I sat in my bedroom struggling to realize I couldn't do it all, I sobbed out a prayer, simple but humbly spoken. "Lord, work through my weakness. I can only get through this by Your strength."

And He was faithful to answer. In His mercy, my mom was visiting, and she shared the load of disinfecting the house, watching the kids, and doing laundry. When friends offered to bring meals, I admitted I needed help and gratefully accepted them. My husband recovered, and the rest of us stayed healthy, almost miraculously. And I was reminded where true strength comes from: God's unlimited power.

Let the gospel give you freedom to admit your weakness and depend on Him.
—ANGELA

Difficult (Yet Dignifying) Counsel

READ 1 TIMOTHY 2:8–15

"I do not permit a woman to teach or to exercise authority over a man." 1 TIMOTHY 2:12

The God-breathed counsel that Paul offered Timothy is a bit challenging to understand. Ok, that's an understatement. This is one of the hardest passages in the New Testament. Not only is it completely out of step with our culture—both the extreme feminist push of previous generations and the push toward "gender-fluidity" in the current generation—but it has several difficult-to-understand phrases. There are about a half-dozen statements that force readers to scratch their heads: *Is Paul against jewelry and hair spray? Why won't he let a woman teach a man? Is Paul suggesting that women are more gullible than men? And, what in the world does Paul mean when he says that women will be "saved through childbearing"?* The simplest way to explain a passage is to paraphrase it. So, here's my paraphrase of Paul's counsel.

[8]Because it's so crucial to pray for the gospel's advance throughout the world, I instruct that the men in the congregation bear the responsibility of leading in prayer every time the church gathers. They should pray with personal fervency and with genuineness—with lives that are marked by love for others rather than by contention, so that their praying isn't hypocritical.

[9]I also instruct the women in the congregation: Their clothing must be appropriate for the occasion and not flashy and distracting—especially not suggestive or tempting in any way. In addition, a Christian woman's temperament should be like her clothing: respectful and controlled, not brazen and ostentatious. Women, don't live as if your beauty is determined by your hairstyle, jewelry, and stylish fashions; it's not! [10]Instead, women who claim to know God should be characterized, first and foremost, by good works—by unselfish sacrificial acts of love for others. A Christlike life is truly beautiful. [11]In the church's general gatherings, Christian women should be learners of gospel truth, not teachers. They should gladly submit themselves to the church's shepherds. [12]Let me be clear: When the whole church gathers, women should not teach or lead the adult men. Instead, they should support the God-called leaders. [13]The reason for my straightforward instruction is deeply rooted in the order of God's good creation: God deliberately created Adam first, Eve second. He gave Adam the responsibility to lead and Eve the responsibility to support Adam. [14]But they caused untold ruin when they inverted God's good order. In the garden, Adam neglected his responsibility to protect Eve, and Eve gave into the temptation. You see, Timothy, awful things happen when men and women try to change their God-given roles. [15]Yet women, who are created by God with a distinctive role from men—most notably, they bear children—will inherit every bit of the glorious salvation God has intended for them if, in fact, they are true Christians. They'll demonstrate their genuineness by their perseverance in faithfulness, love, purity, and self-control. (If you want to further unpack this loaded paragraph, there's no better resource than Tom Schreiner's chapter in *Women in the Church: An Analysis and Application of 1 Timothy 2:9–15*, pp. 85–120.)

In this tough passage, God highly *elevates* your dignity as a woman by focusing on the enduring beauty of your acts of love rather than on the fading beauty of your looks. When you are reminded that your intrinsic worth is not rooted in or even enhanced by your looks, you're exalted (not objectified!). God also elevates your dignity as a woman by focusing you on your creation-given role as a "strong helper" who reflects God Himself (Wendy Alsup, *Is the Bible Good for Women?* p. 57).

Let the gospel restore (not erase!) your God-given dignity and calling.—JOE

Raise Strong Girls

READ PROVERBS 31:10–31

"Strength and dignity are her clothing." PROVERBS 31:25

Having four daughters can change a guy. For me, it has made me appreciate feminine strength. That can show itself in a lot of ways, like in their mother's amazing care for them for the last twenty years. It can also show itself in sports. One of my favorite examples is the athletic career of my firstborn, Rebekah. Her athletics career had an inglorious beginning. During her eighth grade year, she approached me the night before her first game and confided that she was nervous. "I haven't even tried on my costume yet," she lamented. "It's called a uniform, baby," I corrected . . . and lamented. She was so passive on the rare occasions when she got in the game that I finally bribed her: "I'll give you five bucks for every foul you commit!"

Fast forward four years to the championship soccer game for the KHCS Cougars. Bekah had grown into a lock-down defender. She had become so *aggressive*. It was beautiful to behold! Just before halftime she was knocked down by a competitor's elbow to the head. She literally crumbled into a heap. I ran onto the field to see if she was okay. Twenty minutes later, I was giving her Advil and telling her we needed her, as it was a one-goal game. (I know, I know. I'm a terrible person. So much for "Father of the Year.") She played the second half, only later finding out that she had a concussion. Returning was a bad idea. But hey, we won!

The point isn't that your daughters must play sports. It's certainly not that they should play sports with a concussion. The point is that my girls are exceptionally capable. I could list similar examples from academics, music, drama, student body, student legislature, and mission trips. The thing is, there was a time when I (and many, many others) believed that Scripture taught or assumed that women's roles were strictly related to their husbands and children. Their primary virtues were meekness, quietness, and an almost apologetic sweetness. If they went to college, it was to prepare them to be mothers and musicians and homemakers. (I'm exaggerating a bit, but not much.) Truly, many girls are taught that life begins for them when they meet Mr. Right and begin producing Baby Right. It's a problem.

Yes, Scripture commends "a gentle and quiet spirit" (1 Peter 3:4). And yes, Scripture teaches male headship in the home and church (Ephesians 5:22–31; 1 Timothy 2). Without question. But Scripture also gives examples of women who were remarkably strong. The heroic Proverbs 31 woman was kind, but she was also an absolute powerhouse! She manufactured and sold products. She bought real estate. She farmed. She ran a small business. She did charity work. And all the while, she managed her family in a way that honored her husband and protected her kids.

Scripture tells of a strong single businesswoman like Lydia. It praises a married businesswoman and spiritual mentor like Priscilla. It hails an audacious young woman like Queen Esther who saved her people when her older male counterparts could not. Scripture is full of godly women who did exceptional things—often without a husband to "guide" them.

Teach your daughters to be sweet. And teach them to be *strong*. Encourage them to play piano, if they'd like—but also give soccer or acting or debate a try. Challenge them to maximize their mental potential. That may mean no college, which is fine. But it may be college, and grad school or law school or medical school.

Your sweet little girl has a great big brain. Help her find the discipline, confidence, and godly ambition to make the most of it. Such stewardship of her many gifts is biblical. "You go, girl!"

Let the gospel drive you and your girls to attempt great things for God.—CHRIS

Moms are Disciplemakers

READ MATTHEW 10

"Proclaim as you go, saying, 'The kingdom of heaven is at hand.'" MATTHEW 10:7

When King Jesus summons people to follow Him, He doesn't call them to a life of occasional church attendance. He calls them to *be* disciples and to *make* disciples. Making disciples is what Matthew 10 is all about. In this chapter King Jesus actually delegates His authority to every follower, enlisting every Christian as a disciplemaker.

Although the beginning of Jesus' enlistment (vv. 1–16) focuses more narrowly on the original disciples who were called to make disciples in Galilee, it's clear that from verse 17 to the end of the chapter, Jesus' call to make disciples applies to every Christian throughout the rest of church history. (Notice, especially verses 32–42, where Jesus speaks to "everyone" and "whoever," including sons and daughters and daughters-in-law.) So, most of Jesus' instruction here isn't limited to His original disciples, nor is it only for a select group of followers, such as church leaders or those with the gift of teaching. It's for every follower of Jesus, including every Christian mother.

The main thing that Jesus commissions every disciple to do is to "proclaim" that "the kingdom of heaven is at hand" (v. 7). What exactly is this message that you are called to proclaim? It's a message every Christian should know like the back of his or her hand. So, let me give you an open-Bible quiz: Take out a blank sheet of paper, write at the top "The Message of the Kingdom," and write out a simple explanation of that message. After you've tried, read my attempt:

> The message of the kingdom is that God created the earth to be ruled by His chosen King. Soon after God created the world, the first humans chose to reject God's authority. From that point till now, God has subjected His good creation to a cursed existence of suffering and death. But God's curse on creation is actually part of His overall plan to restore it through His chosen King. So, after promising for a few millennia to send His King, God finally sent His only Son Jesus to earth. Throughout His life Jesus proved by His kingly power, wisdom, and generosity that He was the King Who could powerfully undo the curse on creation. But people by and large hated this King and crucified Him. Yet even the King's crucifixion was in perfect keeping with God's plan for world history because Jesus, by His death, can now offer just pardon and kingdom citizenship to any rebel who repents. Jesus rose from the dead and, as King, ascended to heaven where He's now enthroned over the universe. From heaven He will soon return again to earth with terrifying majesty. On the day of His return all the kingdoms of this world will become the kingdom of God's chosen King, Jesus.

What a message! Disciples are called to make disciples with this glorious message. Not every disciple will have the same abilities to proclaim it, the same opportunities to proclaim it, or the same success in proclaiming it, but Jesus expects every disciple to faithfully speak this message to others, even others who may oppose us. And, in the heart of the passage, Jesus assumes that Christians will share it with family members (that includes Christian moms telling God's kingdom story to their kids) (v. 21).

Parenting is nothing less than discipleship. And at the heart of discipleship is consistent proclamation of the awesome message that Jesus is God's chosen, crucified, risen, and returning King.

Let proclaiming the gospel be at the heart of your mission as a mom. —JOE

Don't Lose Hope

READ ACTS 13:1–13 AND 15:36–41

"Get Mark and bring him with you, for he is very useful to me for ministry." 2 TIMOTHY 4:10

I have two older brothers, Jeff and Dan. By God's grace, all three of us are in vocational ministry. Jeff pastored for twenty-five years and now serves as the Director of International Bible Conference, a ministry that teaches expositional preaching to pastors around the world. Dan was a church planter in Brazil for thirteen years. For the last decade, he has served as the Director for Brazil Gospel Fellowship Mission. I have pastored for over two decades, first as a church planter in Ohio and now as a pastor in Atlanta. God has been good to my family!

Now, because we're all preachers, some assume that we sat around preaching to one another and praying together as children. Nothing could be further from the truth. We were rascals! As boys we started several fires—including one that led Dad to call the police after finding out we had lied to the firefighters who put it out. I was four, but certain that I was headed to Alcatraz. Later, we got caught smoking cigarettes; I was five. Dad went "vigilante" that time, locking us in the shed until we had smoked the rest of the pack. It worked! By the time I was twelve I had been drunk with alcohol and stoned with marijuana. Our juvenile delinquency wasn't always that spectacular, but it was certainly there. Yet, by God's grace, we're all serving the Lord today and raising our children to do the same. What happened? What lessons can you learn from delinquents-turned-disciples?

Withhold judgment until adulthood. Parents often think they're either successes or failures in the toddler years. Get off to a good start. Pray like crazy. But you won't know how your kids have turned out for a long time. Resist the urge to congratulate yourself for a "well-behaved" pre-teen. I've seen a heartbreaking number of "model kids" run fast and furiously from home when they turned eighteen. Likewise resist the urge to condemn yourself for a "not-so-well-behaved" child or teen. I've seen a heartwarming number of "trouble kids" return zealously to the faith their parents taught them. Don't shrug off their disobedience. Discipline them. Teach them. Love them. Pray for them. But don't believe the lie that your child's character and destiny are forged by age thirteen. Give grace a chance to do something amazing.

Rejoice that failure need not be final. Take heart from the example of John Mark, the son of Mary, the sister of Barnabas. Her son began well and was chosen as a team member for the very first mission trip in church history (13:1–5). Sadly, he cratered. Big time. He abandoned Paul and Barnabas and returned home (13:13). Paul was finished with him. Barnabas, ever the encourager, wanted to give him another chance. The "dream team" of Paul and Barnabas disagreed so sharply that they split up (15:36–41). We're not told what his mother's response was, but it must have included grief and worry. Thankfully, John Mark came around. His failure wasn't final. God kept working on him, even when Paul didn't. In time, he was useful to Paul. In time he accompanied Peter in ministry, wrote a Gospel, and died as a martyr. Don't be quick to write off a challenging child.

Take necessary steps when you see that what you're doing isn't working. Optimism is not a strategy. My parents took a drastic step to help their wayward boys. They moved our family an hour away—not for business or traffic, but so we'd be close to a church with a strong youth group. They uprooted and inconvenienced themselves to save their rebellious sons. And it changed our lives.

Don't give up. Don't write your prodigal off. Consider making a change. Pray. Be patient. And watch God do something amazing with your child for His glory.

Let the gospel be the lens through which you view your rebellious child.—CHRIS

What's Your Definition of Greatness?

READ MATTHEW 20:17-28

"Whoever would be great among you must be your servant." MATTHEW 20:26

In today's passage the mother of James and John—I'll call her "Mrs. Z"—approaches Jesus with a request (v. 20). She wants her sons, who have been Jesus' disciples from the beginning, to be great. It's interesting that, when Mrs. Z makes the request, Jesus responds not to her but to her boys (vv. 21–22). I think that's because Jesus knows that the ambitious boys put their mother up to this. In other words, not only does Mrs. Z want her sons to be great, but the sons themselves want to be great. We find out later that all the disciples were angry *at James and John* for making this request (v. 24). And, the other disciples were ticked off, not because they were spiritually concerned for the evident weakness of James and John, but because they were *envious*. James and John beat them to asking the question!

Do you want to be great in the eyes of King Jesus? Do you want to be a great mom? Do you want to raise great children? I hope so! I hope you pray every day that God would be glorified in you and your children. It's crucial, however, that you have a Christ-shaped understanding of greatness. The disciples thought like the world: A great life is a life that's more important and more significant than the lives of those around me. With that definition, everything in life becomes a competition for preeminence: *How do I compare at school, among friends, at church, among fellow parents, among neighbors?* Worldly greatness is being regarded as superior to others.

But that's not Jesus' definition. For Jesus greatness is a life that unselfishly serves others. That's the point of today's reading in which Jesus calls every one of His followers to seek to be the greatest servant—to want to be the slave (vv. 26–27). That's the essence of Christlike leadership in every sphere of life, whether in business, in the church, or at home. J. Oswald Sanders explains in his classic book, *Spiritual Leadership*:

> Jesus was a revolutionary . . . in His teaching on leadership. The term *servant* speaks everywhere of low prestige, low respect, low honor. Most people are not attracted to such a low-value role. When Jesus used the term, however, it was a synonym for greatness. (p. 21)

Jesus motivates your pursuit of greatness by pointing to His own example. Jesus is "the Son of Man" (v. 28), a title that refers to the Individual chosen by God to have the highest authority on earth (Daniel 7:13–14). Yet, Jesus says that the Son of Man did *not* come to be served. That's incredible. The Person with highest authority didn't come to be waited on by assistants, groomers, wardrobe specialists, speechwriters, drivers, pilots, cooks, groundskeepers, lawyers, and financial managers. He came to serve—in fact, to free slaves by dying in their place (v. 28). In other words, the highest Authority on earth chose to be the Servant of slaves. What glory!

So, what picture comes to your mind when you imagine a great mom? What's your dream of greatness? Is it that your children stand out at school or in life? Is it that your family stands out as being particularly happy or as "having it together" more than most? If those are your dreams, you probably live with feelings of superiority or depression—both of which are ungodly. Jesus is in the business of overhauling your dreams as much as He overhauled the dreams of Mrs. Z and her sons. Christian mom, here's some good news: Jesus knows you, He loves you, and He's going to keep shaping your vision to match His. He'll lovingly lead you to increasingly say, "I just want to be a servant. I want to be a servant-minded mom who faithfully raises servant-minded children." Because greatness equals faithfully serving others.

Let the gospel shape your ambition for greatness.—JOE

Spoiled Daughters

READ MATTHEW 7

"Ask, and it shall be given to you; seek, and you will find." MATTHEW 7:7

My daughter has those big brown eyes. Mine are blue-green and never quite certain which they want to be. Blue-green eyes aren't any good for begging; brown eyes were made for it. And my daughter has them, inherited from both her father and her great-grandmother. Big, brown, eager, expectant eyes. Eyes that melt her father's heart.

I don't think my husband plays favorites among our three children, but like any daddy who loves his daughter, he has a particular weakness toward her and those brown eyes. And she, as a result, has a particular confidence and boldness that comes, not from being spoiled, but from knowing his love.

When she was younger, she would come to him, climb into his lap at no invitation, and draw him into her world of fairy princesses and delightful impossibilities. She knows no fear, no boundaries, no limits to his acceptance. And why should she? Isn't this the man who comforts her, carries her on his strong shoulders, and works to fulfill her needs? Isn't this the man who rescues her from bugs, big dogs, her brothers, and thunderstorms? Even his correction confirms that she belongs to him.

In Matthew 7:9 Jesus uses a father's love for his child to explain how much greater our heavenly Father's love is for us. "Which one of you," He asks, "if his son [or daughter] asks him for bread, will give him a stone? Or if he asks for a fish, will give him a serpent? If you then, who are evil, know how to give good gifts to your children, how much more will your Father who is in heaven give good things to those who ask him!"

The promise that God is a good Father who gives good things to His children doesn't mean He automatically grants everything we want. He is a *good* Father, after all—One who knows what is best for us and gives accordingly. But I worry that sometimes we think our wanting something automatically means He *won't* give it to us, that He will withhold it from us to teach us a lesson. And so we never ask. But in so doing, we misjudge the generous heart of God.

After all, which father among you, if his daughter looks at him with her big brown eyes and asks for a good gift would be unmoved by it? And if we as earthly parents are moved by our children's requests, how dare we presume that God, our heavenly Father, is any less kind?

Once when his wife Susannah unexpectedly received a songbird as a gift—something she had been secretly praying for—C. H. Spurgeon teased her, saying, "I think you are one of your heavenly Father's spoiled children, and He just gives you whatever you ask for" (*The Autobiography of Charles H. Spurgeon*, p. 185).

Yes, I suppose we are all spoiled children. Children who can ask because they know it will be given. Children who can seek because they know they will find. Children who can knock because the door will be opened to them. Children who can come boldly to our heavenly Father, not because of our goodness, but because of His. Because Christ has made a way, we can draw near our Father's throne with confidence, "that we may receive mercy and find grace to help in time of need" (Hebrews 4:16).

Let the gospel give you the confidence to ask God to give you good gifts.

—HANNAH

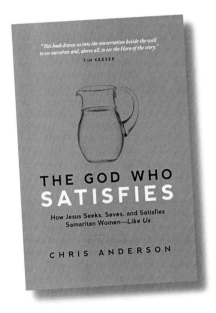
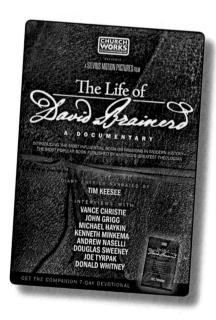

OTHER TITLES IN THIS SERIES

Gospel Meditations for Women

"Wrestling with guilt and frustration, far too many Christian women are living below the privileges of their spiritual inheritance. The solution is not found in any strengthened resolve of duty, but rather in having souls settled in the blessed liberty of Christ through the sweet enjoyment of the gospel. A union of sound doctrine and practical teaching, *Gospel Meditations for Women* beautifully highlights those unbinding messages of grace that so powerfully ignite joyful passion for Christ and holy living. What an invaluable resource!"

—**Holly Stratton**, conference speaker and blogger at *LifeHurts.us*

Gospel Meditations for Men

"A model of robust biblical thinking, this little book is gospel gold, an ample treasury for men who long to renew their minds and be transformed by the mighty themes of the gospel."

—**Milton Vincent**, author of *A Gospel Primer for Christians* and pastor of Cornerstone Fellowship Bible Church, Riverside, California

Gospel Meditations for Missions

"By almost any standard—the intentionality of local churches to train, assess, and prepare prospective missionaries; the length of time it takes a missionary to raise support; the little sense of gospel partnership we have with the missionaries we do support—Western Christians don't do missions very well. The reason we don't do missions well is that we've not thought about missions well. This book has our poor thinking about missions in its crosshairs."

—**Matthew Hoskinson**, pastor of The First Baptist Church in New York City and author of *Assurance of Salvation*

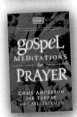

Gospel Meditations for Prayer

"Brief and biblical, these meditations are full of sharp edges. They lead us to pray as cross-bearing disciples of Christ. Yet Anderson, Tyrpak, and Trueman comfort us with Christ's perfect grace for fallen people. So *Gospel Meditations for Prayer* is an encouraging book, but one designed to stretch you."

—**Joel Beeke**, president of Puritan Reformed Theological Seminary, Grand Rapids, and editor of *Taking Hold of God: Reformed and Puritan Perspectives on Prayer*

Gospel Meditations for the Hurting

"These meditations are Word-centered prescriptions that blow away the meaningless Christian platitudes often used to mask unanswerable pain. Until that day when Christ Himself wipes away all tears from our eyes, the Scriptures provide strength, help, and hope in this broken world. Let this book guide you to Christ, the only sure and lasting Refuge."

—**Tim Keesee**, author of the *Dispatches from the Front* DVD series and book and executive director of Frontline Missions International

Gospel Meditations for Christmas

"This work is more than a mere devotional and collection of meditations for Christmas. These meditations are a mini Christology. I hope they will be read far beyond December. There is too much truth here to be relegated to the Christmas season alone. I highly recommend this work for your greater understanding and worship of Jesus Christ."

—**Rick Holland**, pastor of Mission Road Bible Church, Kansas City, and professor of Homiletics at The Expositor's Seminary